I0815517

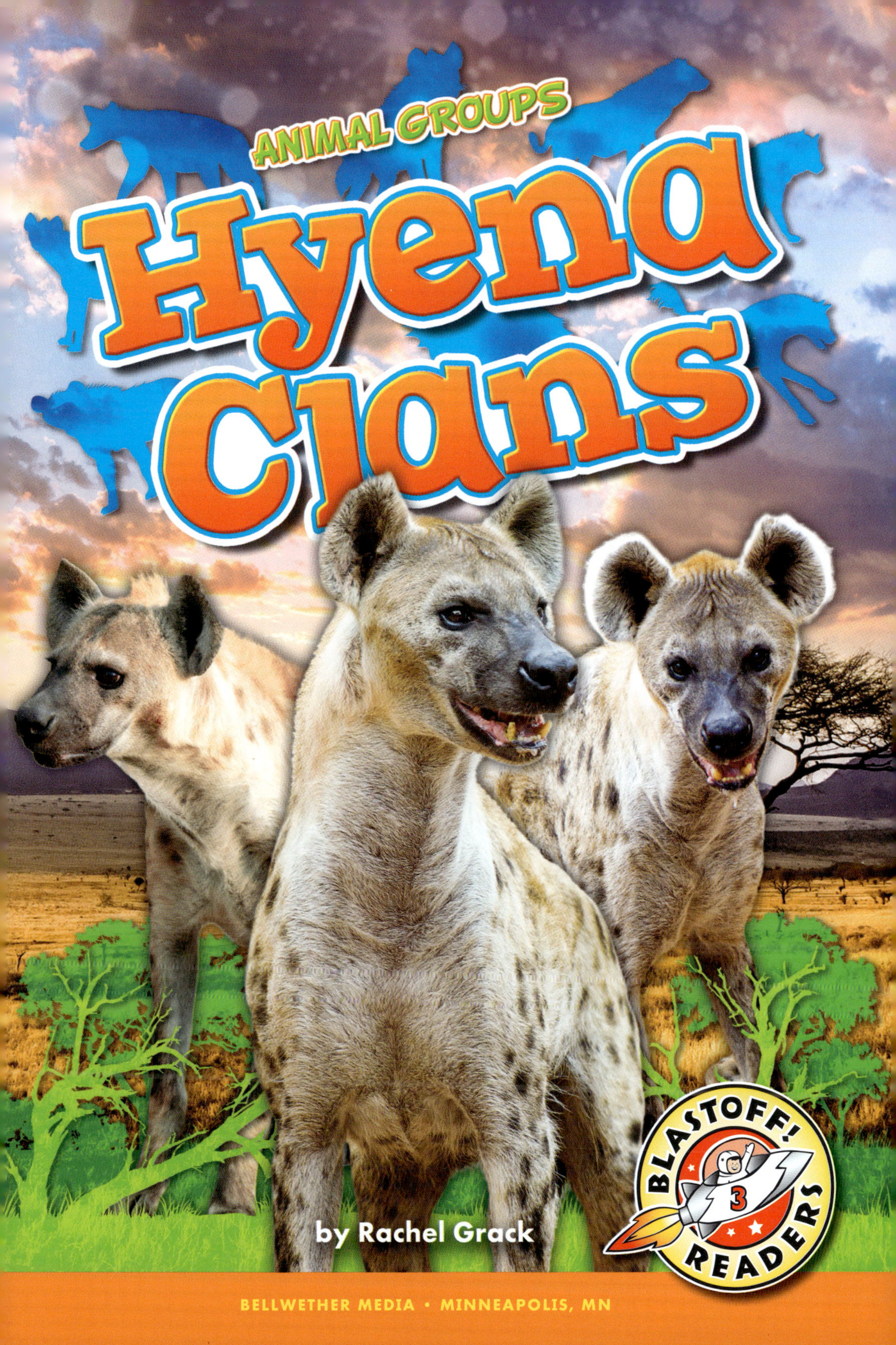

Animal Groups
Hyena Clans
by Rachel Grack
Blastoff! Readers 3
Bellwether Media • Minneapolis, MN

Blastoff! Readers are carefully developed by literacy experts to build reading stamina and move students toward fluency by combining standards-based content with developmentally appropriate text.

Level 1 provides the most support through repetition of high-frequency words, light text, predictable sentence patterns, and strong visual support.

Level 2 offers early readers a bit more challenge through varied sentences, increased text load, and text-supportive special features.

Level 3 advances early-fluent readers toward fluency through increased text load, less reliance on photos, advancing concepts, longer sentences, and more complex special features.

★ **Blastoff! Universe**

Reading Level

Grade K

Grades 1–3

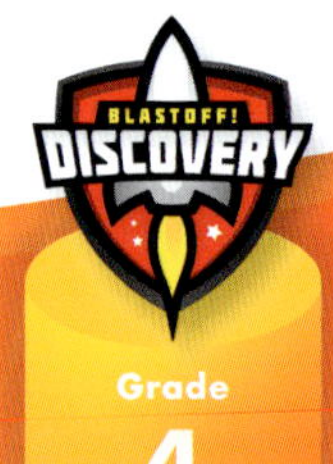

Grade 4

This edition first published in 2026 by Bellwether Media, Inc.

Library of Congress Cataloging-in-Publication Data

LC record for Hyena Clans available at: https://lccn.loc.gov/2025018607

Editor: Suzane Nguyen   Designer: Brittany McIntosh

Printed in the United States of America, North Mankato, MN.

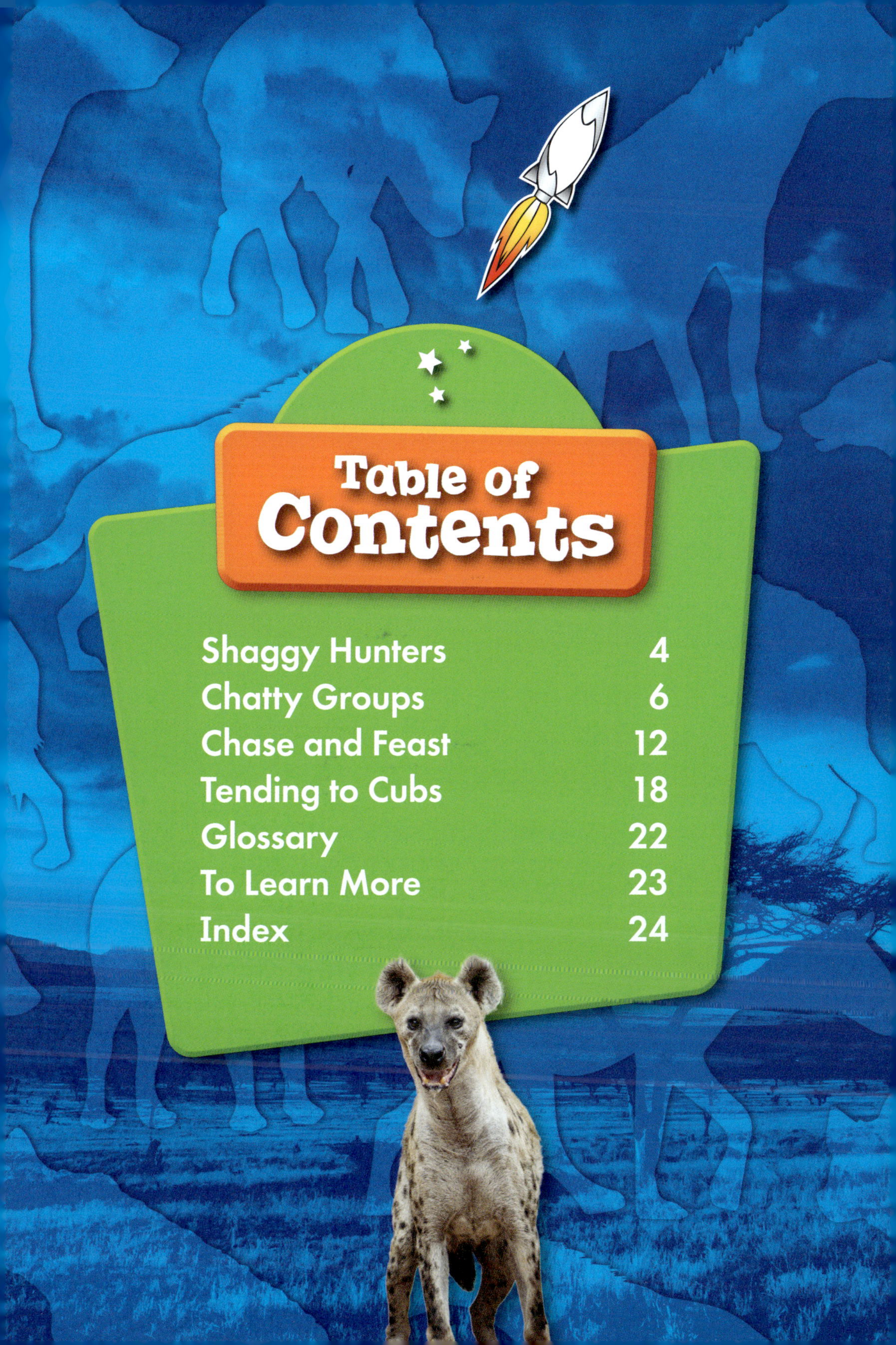

Table of Contents

Shaggy Hunters	4
Chatty Groups	6
Chase and Feast	12
Tending to Cubs	18
Glossary	22
To Learn More	23
Index	24

Shaggy Hunters

spotted hyena clan

Hyenas are shaggy **mammals** that look like wild dogs. There are four different **species**. Spotted hyenas are the largest and most common.

Hyenas live in groups called clans. They hunt on the **savannas** of Africa.

Chatty Groups

Hyena clans can have around 80 members. An **alpha female** leads each clan. Her **offspring** rank just below her.

Male hyenas join from other clans. They earn their place in the new clan.

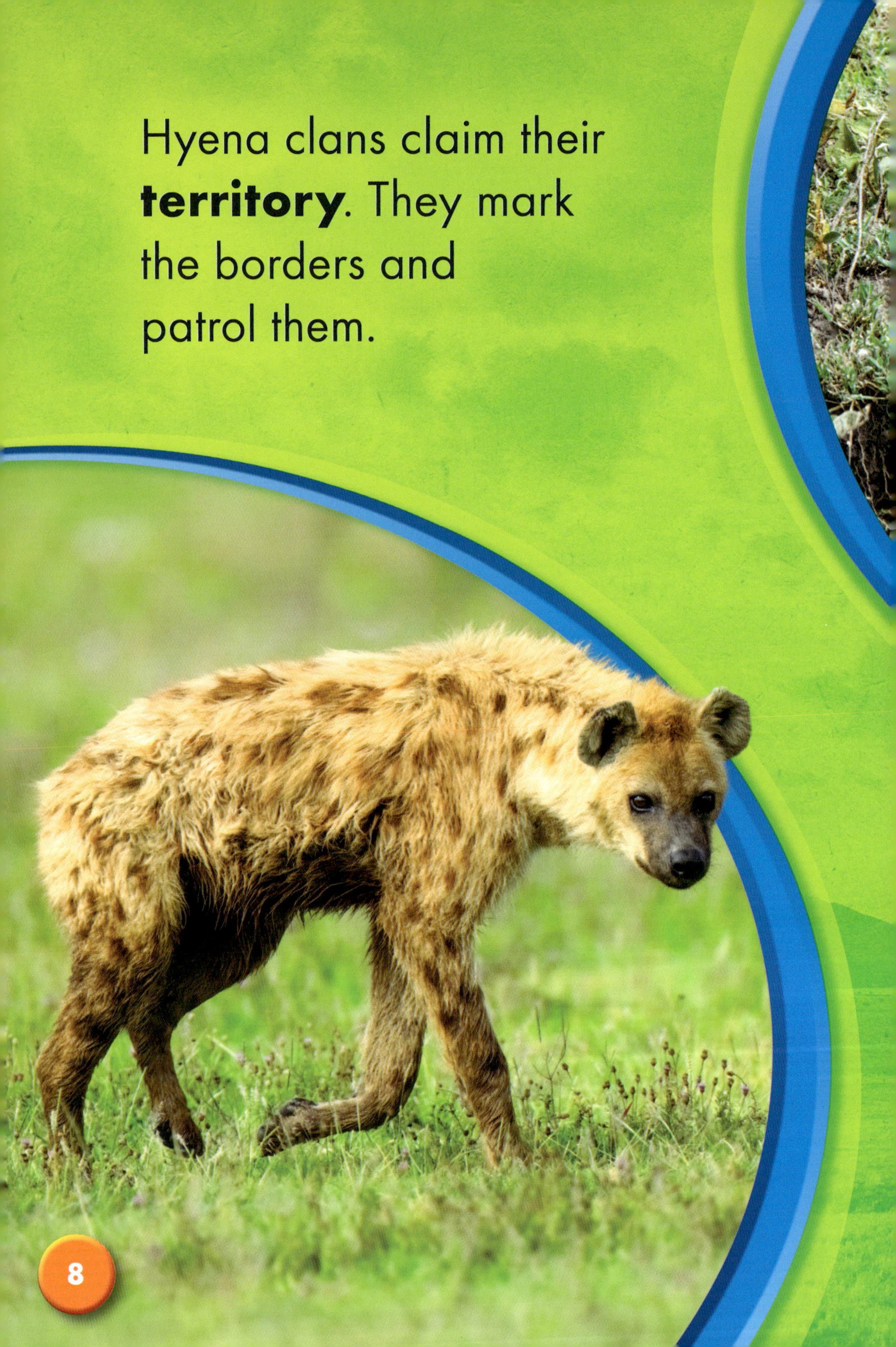

Hyena clans claim their **territory**. They mark the borders and patrol them.

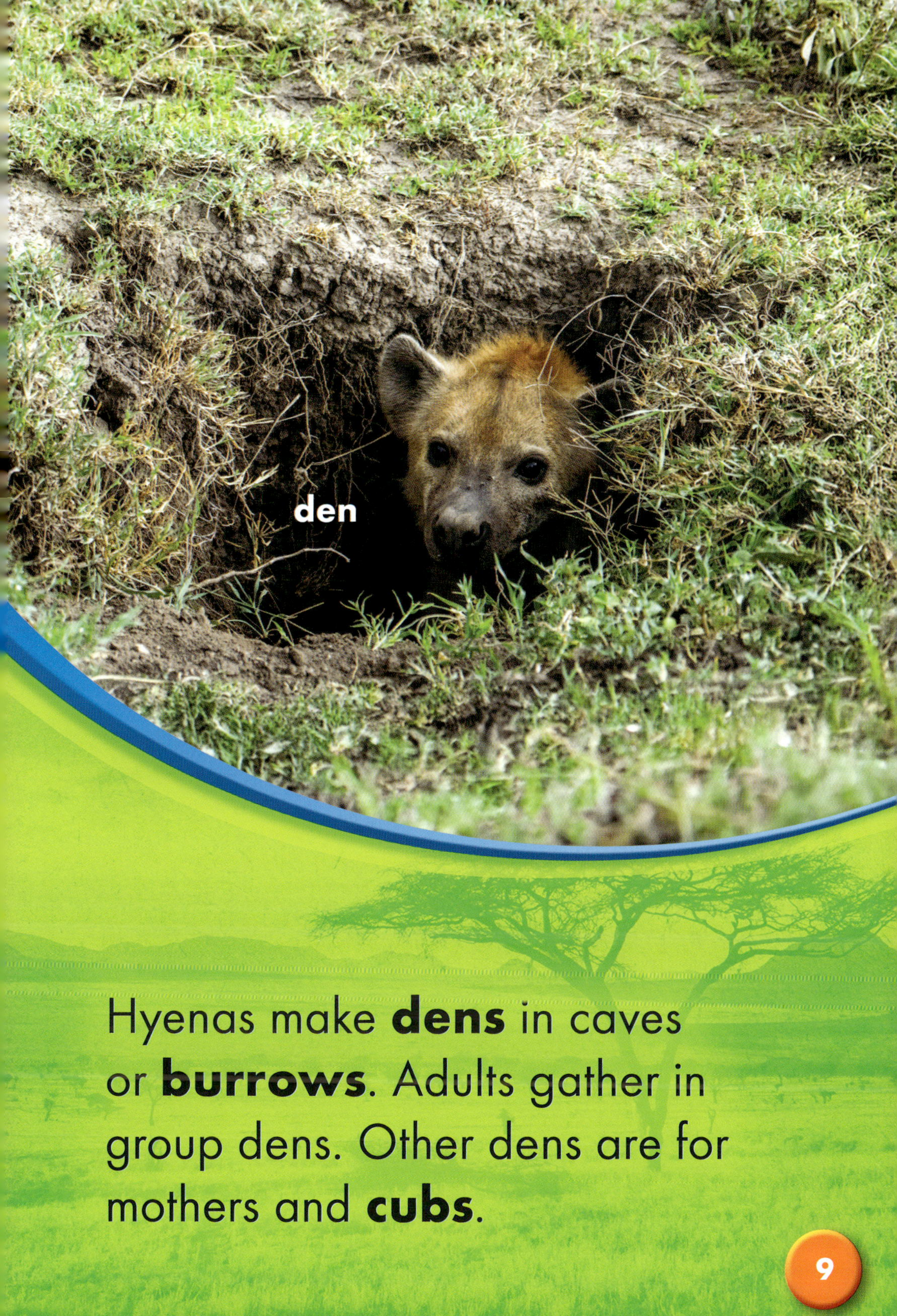

Hyenas make **dens** in caves or **burrows**. Adults gather in group dens. Other dens are for mothers and **cubs**.

Hyena clans are chatty. They greet one another with groans and squeals. They laugh when they are nervous or upset.

Hyenas fold down their ears when scared. They show their teeth when **aggressive**.

Chase and Feast

Hyenas are **carnivores**. Hyena clans work together to catch **prey**.

They separate an animal from its **herd**. Hyenas chase prey until it gets tired. Then, the hyenas attack and eat.

Working Together

separate a weak, old, or young animal

chase prey until it is tired

attack together

eat

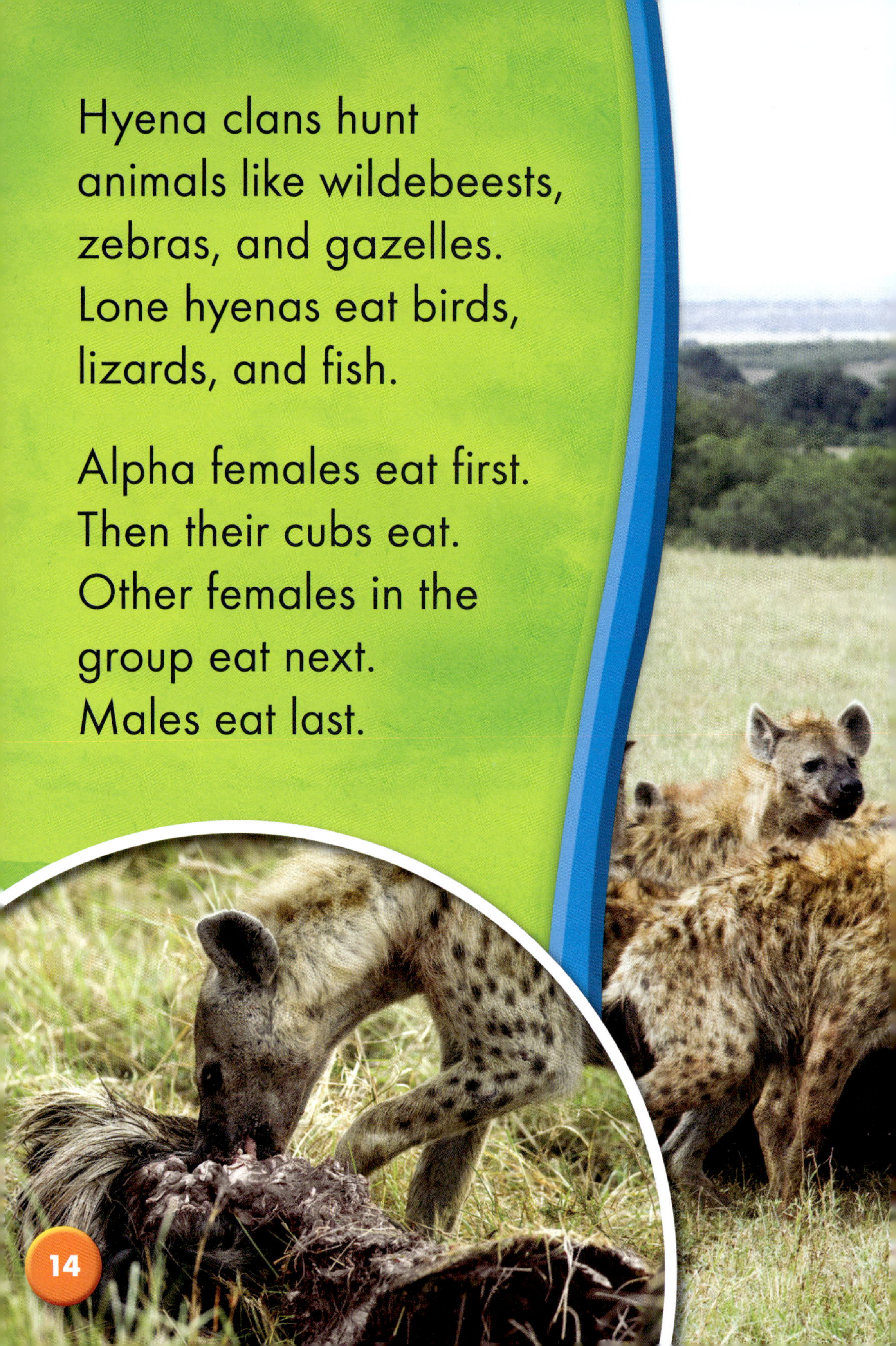

Hyena clans hunt animals like wildebeests, zebras, and gazelles. Lone hyenas eat birds, lizards, and fish.

Alpha females eat first. Then their cubs eat. Other females in the group eat next. Males eat last.

Hyena Diet
wildebeests
zebras
gazelles

Hyenas are **apex predators**. But some clans share hunting grounds with lions.

Lions can take down hyenas to steal food. Hyenas will make a laughing sound to call other clan members to help defend food.

Tending to Cubs

cubs

Mothers have cubs in their own birth dens. Most **litters** have two to four cubs. Mothers stay with their newborn cubs.

Later, mothers bring cubs together in a shared den.

Mothers sometimes go on hunts. Other hyenas watch over their cubs.

Female cubs often stay with their clans as adults. Adult males often join new clans!

Glossary

aggressive—showing a readiness to fight

alpha female—the most powerful and high-ranking female animal in a group

apex predators—animals at the top of the food chain that are not preyed upon by other animals

burrows—tunnels or holes in the ground used as an animal's home

carnivores—animals that only eat meat

cubs—baby hyenas

dens—sheltered places

herd—a group of animals that lives and travels together

litters—groups of cubs born at the same time

mammals—warm-blooded animals that have backbones and feed their young milk

offspring—the young of a male and female pair

prey—animals that are hunted by other animals for food

savannas—flat grasslands with few trees

species—kinds of animals

territory—the land area where an animal lives

To Learn More

AT THE LIBRARY

Barth, Kelley. *A Cackle of Hyenas.* Parker, Colo.: The Child's World, 2024.

Gendell, Megan. *Spotted Hyenas.* Mendota Heights, Minn.: Apex Editions, 2024.

Gillespie, Katie. *Hyena.* New York, N.Y.: Lightbox Learning, 2023.

ON THE WEB

FACTSURFER

Factsurfer.com gives you a safe, fun way to find more information.

1. Go to www.factsurfer.com.
2. Enter "hyena clans" into the search box and click 🔍.
3. Select your book cover to see a list of related content.

Index

Africa, 5
alpha female, 6, 14
apex predators, 16
carnivores, 12
clans, 4, 5, 6, 7, 8, 10, 12, 14, 16, 17, 20
communication, 10, 11, 17
cubs, 9, 14, 18, 19, 20
dens, 9, 18, 19
ears, 11
food, 14, 15, 17
groans, 10
hunt, 5, 14, 16, 20
laughs, 10, 17
lions, 16, 17
litters, 18
males, 7, 14, 20
mammals, 4
mothers, 9, 18, 19, 20
offspring, 6
prey, 12, 13
range, 5
savannas, 5
species, 4
squeals, 10
teeth, 11
territory, 8
working together, 13

The images in this book are reproduced through the courtesy of: Anan Kaewkhammul, front cover (left hyena); Krakenimages.com, front cover (middle hyena, right hyena), p. 3; Maciej Czekajewski, front cover (background); Robert Muckley/ Getty Images, pp. 4-5; Gunter, p. 6; neurobit, p. 7; KenCanning, p. 8; robertharding/ Alamy Stock Photo, p. 9; Alison Mees, pp. 10-11; VisualStories, p. 11; Uwe Skrzypczak/ Alamy Stock Photo, p. 12; Maurizio Bersanelli, p. 13 (step 1); Frederick Mark Sheridan-Johnson/ Alamy Stock Photo, p. 13 (step 2); Juergen Ritterbach/ Alamy Stock Photo, p. 13 (step 3); Henk Bogaard, p. 13 (step 4); James, p. 14; Abdelrahman Hassanein, pp. 14-15; EcoPrint, p. 15 (wildebeests); francesco de marco, p. 15 (zebras); Milan Zygmunt, p. 15 (gazelles); Tempura, p. 16; MintImages, p. 17; ondrejprosicky, p. 18; Michele Burgess, p. 19; Vladislav T. Jirousek, p. 20; guenterguni, pp. 20-21; reptiles4all, p. 23.